HORSES

The AMERICAN QUARTER Horse

by Amanda Parise-Peterson

Consultant:
American Quarter Horse Youth Association
Amarillo, Texas

Capstone press
Mankato, Minnesota

Edge Books are published by Capstone Press,
151 Good Counsel Drive, P.O. Box 669, Mankato, Minnesota 56002.
www.capstonepress.com

Library of Congress Cataloging-in-Publication Data
Parise-Peterson, Amanda.
    The American quarter horse / by Amanda Parise-Peterson.
    p. cm.—(Edge books. Horses)
    Includes bibliographical references (p. 31) and index.
    ISBN 0-7368-3764-7 (hardcover)
    1. Quarter horse—Juvenile literature. I. Title. II. Series.
SF293.Q3P37 2005
636.1'33—dc22   2004019419

Summary: Describes American Quarter Horses, including their history, physical
features, and primary uses.

Editorial Credits
Angie Kaelberer, editor; Juliette Peters, designer; Deirdre Barton,
    photo researcher; Scott Thoms, photo editor

Photo Credits
Capstone Press/Gary Sundermeyer, 8, 13, 25
Courtesy of the American Quarter Horse Association, 26, 27
Courtesy of the National Museum of Racing and Hall of Fame, 9
John Blasdel, 17
Karen Patterson, back cover, 29
Library of Congress, 6
Mane Photo/Jennay Hitesman, cover
Nancy McCallum Photography/Nancy M. McCallum, 14–15
Paula da Silva, 12, 23
Prophoto by Lori, 5, 11, 18
Sharon P. Fibelkorn, 24
Timothy Johnson, 20

1 2 3 4 5 6 10 09 08 07 06 05

Table of Contents

FEATURES

Chapter 1

Calm Companions

People sometimes call the American Quarter Horse the golden retriever of the horse world. Like golden retriever dogs, Quarter Horses are calm, loyal, and cooperative.

Quarter Horses do well in many areas. They herd cattle on ranches and perform at rodeos. People also use Quarter Horses for trail riding, racing, and shows.

Learn about:
★ **North America's first horses**
★ **Beginning of the breed**
★ **Early ancestors**

American Quarter Horses are prized for their strength and gentleness.

In the late 1800s, cowboys used Quarter Horses for ranch work.

American Horses

Before 1519, no horses lived in North America. That year, Spanish explorer Hernán Cortés brought horses to Mexico. The European explorers and settlers who followed Cortés also brought horses.

Settlers traded horses to American Indians. Trading helped the horses spread to what is now Texas, New Mexico, and California.

Breeding

In the 1600s and 1700s, English settlers brought Hobby and Thoroughbred horses to North America. People bred the sleek Thoroughbreds and muscular Hobbies to North American horses. The offspring were the first American Quarter Horses.

Quarter Horses quickly became popular with settlers. The smart, sturdy horses herded cattle, provided transportation, and helped clear land for farms. They also ran fast. Many of them won quarter-mile (.4-kilometer) races. Quarter Horses were named after this distance.

Official Breed

In 1940, the American Quarter Horse became an official horse breed. That year, several Quarter Horse owners formed the American Quarter Horse Association (AQHA) in Amarillo, Texas. The AQHA started a registry for Quarter Horse breeding records.

Today, Quarter Horses are among the most popular horses in the world. They are found in at least 80 countries and have the world's largest breed registry. About 3 million horses are registered with the AQHA.

Important Ancestors

Janus was an important Quarter Horse ancestor. This chestnut horse was born in England in 1746. Ten years later, his owner brought him to the Virginia colony.

Janus looked different from other horses at the time. He was large-boned and compact. His muscular back legs helped him run fast. Janus' owner bred him to many mares. Janus passed on his qualities to his foals.

Sir Archy and Shiloh were also important to the Quarter Horse breed. Sir Archy was a champion racehorse who sired at least 300 champion foals. One of his descendants, Shiloh, became a famous racehorse in Texas.

In the 1850s, people called Steel Dust the fastest horse in Texas. He was so popular that many people called early Quarter Horses "Steel Dusts."

Sir Archy

Chapter 2

America's Workhorse

Quarter Horses have large, muscular body frames. Their firm, strong bodies give Quarter Horses a straight stride. Their build also helps them move quickly and lightly.

Strong hindquarters give Quarter Horses their speed. The muscular hindquarters thrust them forward from standing into a fast run.

Quarter Horses have short, wide heads. Their ears are small. The eyes are large and alert.

Quarter Horses have small muzzles and large nostrils. Their nostrils help them breathe quickly and deeply while running.

Learn about:
★ Body type
★ Colors
★ Personality

American Quarter Horses are large and muscular.

A Colorful Breed

Quarter Horses can be one of 16 color patterns. The most common color is sorrel, which is red-brown. Other common colors are black, chestnut, brown, and gray.

▼ Many Quarter Horses are sorrel in color.

Chestnut horses are a shade of copper or red. Dun, buckskin, and red dun are all shades of brown.

Quarter Horses can be bay, palomino, or grullo. Bay horses are dark brown with black manes and tails. A palomino is tan with a lighter mane and tail. Grullos are gray. Their manes and tails are black.

Roan is another color pattern found in Quarter Horses. Roan horses have white hairs mixed with hair of a darker color.

Cremello and perlino are less common color patterns. Both cremellos and perlinos have pink skin, white or cream-colored coats, and blue eyes.

Calm and Quiet

Quarter Horses are known for their cooperative personalities. They are calm and gentle. They work hard to please their owners.

Quarter Horses are willing and able to do many jobs. They herd cattle, pull carts and wagons, and carry riders on their backs.

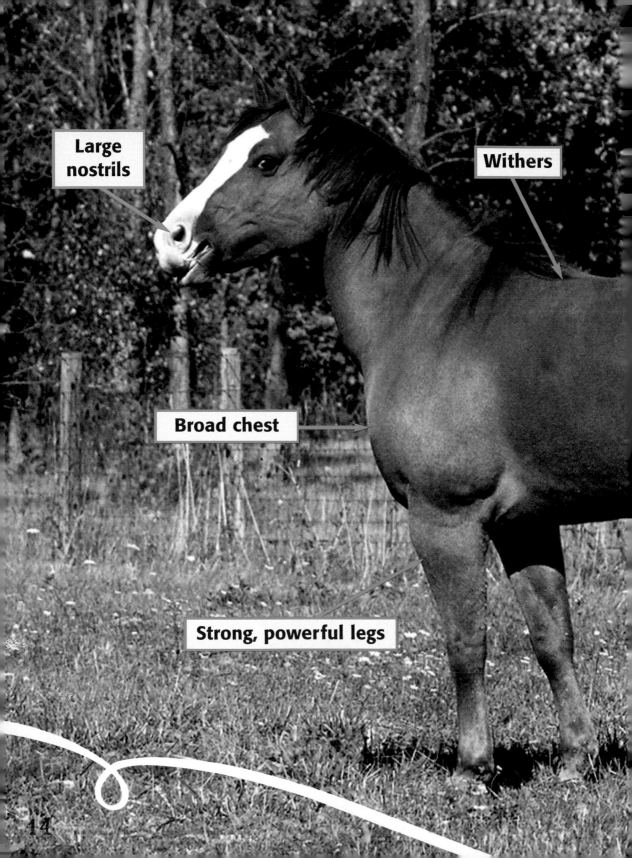

Large nostrils

Withers

Broad chest

Strong, powerful legs

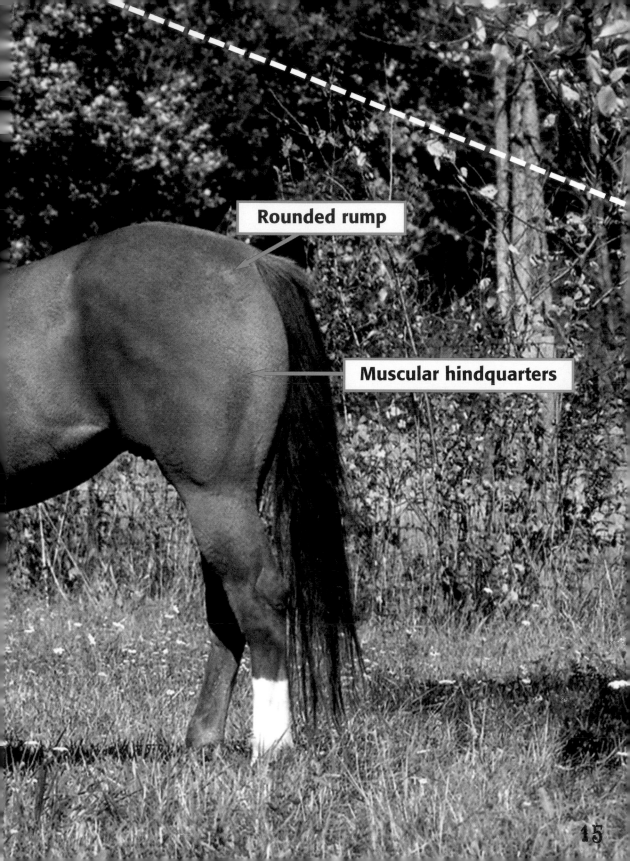

Rounded rump

Muscular hindquarters

15

Chapter 3

Stars of the Rodeo

People still race Quarter Horses and use them to herd cattle. Many Quarter Horses also compete in rodeos. Rodeo events test the skills of horses and riders. The events require teamwork and speed.

Rodeos

Beginning in the mid-1800s, cowboys made money by rounding up huge herds of roaming cattle. For fun, the cowboys held contests in roping cattle and other ranch skills. People started calling the contests rodeos. Quarter Horses became one of the most popular breeds to use in rodeos.

Learn about:
- ★ Early rodeos
- ★ Events
- ★ Training

Some rodeo events test the horse's ability to work with cattle.

Riders try not to knock down barrels as they race.

Rodeos are still a way for horses and riders to show off their herding skills. The events test the horse and rider's skill with cattle.

Rodeo Events

At barrel races, three barrels are set up in the arena in the pattern of a triangle.

Horses race in a cloverleaf pattern around the barrels. The best barrel racing runs take only about 17 seconds. Judges add 5 seconds for each barrel knocked to the ground.

During most rodeo events, the fastest time wins. In saddle bronc and bareback riding, the longest time wins. The rider must stay on the bucking horse for a certain number of seconds.

Horses chase a calf or steer during roping events. In tie-down roping events, the rider gets off the horse and ties the cow's legs together. In dally team roping, another rider throws a rope around the cow's back legs. Both riders wrap the ropes twice around the saddle horns. The horses then quickly stop and pull back on the ropes to keep the animal under control.

Well-trained Quarter Horses match their speed to the cattle's speed. The horses make quick changes in direction. The rider can then focus on roping the calf or steer.

Two or more riders work together during team roping events.

PRCA

The Professional Rodeo Cowboys Association (PRCA) is the largest rodeo organization in the United States. Each year, the PRCA sponsors nearly 30 large rodeos throughout the country. It awards prize money to the winners. In December, the top riders end the rodeo season with the National Finals Rodeo in Las Vegas, Nevada.

Teamwork

Training for rodeos takes time and practice. Riders and their Quarter Horses must learn to work as a team. The horses should respond quickly to commands from their riders. Riders use their legs, reins, body positions, and voices to give signals to the horses.

Some Quarter Horses are better suited for certain events. For example, not all Quarter Horses make good barrel racing horses. They must be quick and have excellent balance to race around the barrels.

Chapter 4

Quarter Horses in Action

Quarter Horses are still used to herd cattle on ranches. Many Quarter Horses race or compete in horse shows. Quarter Horses also are good choices for trail riding and other pleasure riding.

Quarter Horse Shows

The American Quarter Horse Association sponsors many horse shows in the United States each year. Each November, the AQHA holds the World Championship. The show lasts for 15 days and awards a total of about $2 million in money and other prizes to the winners.

Learn about:
- ★ Shows
- ★ Western competitions
- ★ Races

American Quarter Horses make excellent pleasure riding horses.

In horsemanship events, the rider and horse should move together smoothly.

At the World Championship, top horses compete for the Silver Spur award. The AQHA gives this award each year to the horse that best represents the breed.

Western Performance

Western performance competitions include horse show and rodeo events. Western pleasure and horsemanship are show events. Rodeo events include reining and team penning.

In Western pleasure events, riders guide their horses at a slow pace around the show ring. The horses walk, jog, and lope. Judges score them on appearance and ability. In horsemanship events, judges rate the rider's abilities.

Reining and Penning

In reining events, riders guide their horses through exercises such as spins and sliding stops. During sliding stops, horses run at full speed. They dig their back feet into the ground and slide to a stop.

Team penning is the fastest growing Western performance event. Three riders rely on their horses' "cow sense" to separate three marked cattle from a herd. The riders chase the marked cattle into a pen.

Racing

The quarter-mile is still the most popular distance for Quarter Horses to race. Top Quarter Horses run a quarter-mile in about 21 seconds. They reach speeds of 55 miles (89 kilometers) per hour.

⬇ In reining events, a horse slides to a stop at its rider's command.

Quarter-mile races are held at racetracks all over North America. Many races also take place at state and county fairs.

The American Quarter Horse has been prized for years for its gentle personality and hardworking nature. This "golden retriever" of the horse world will keep winning new fans and friends in the future.

Quarter Horses can run a quarter mile in 21 seconds.

Fast Facts:
The American Quarter Horse

Name: American Quarter Horses get their name from quarter-mile races.

History: The breed began in North America in the 1700s. The American Quarter Horse became an official breed in 1940.

Height: Quarter Horses are 15 or 16 hands (about 5 feet or 1.5 meters) tall at the withers. Each hand equals 4 inches (10 centimeters).

Weight: 1,200 to 1,500 pounds (540 to 680 kilograms)

Colors: Quarter Horses can be one of 16 color patterns. Common colors are sorrel, chestnut, bay, black, brown, gray, and roan.

Features: muscular hindquarters; long legs; short, broad head; small muzzle; large nostrils

Personality: calm, cooperative, gentle

Abilities: Quarter Horses are excellent all-around horses. They are the most common horses used for ranch work and rodeos. They are also good choices for trail riding, racing, and shows.

Life span: 20 to 30 years

Glossary

ancestor (AN-sess-tur)—a member of a breed that lived a long time ago

foal (FOHL)—a horse that is less than 1 year old

Hobby (HAW-bee)—a small horse breed that began in Ireland

mare (MAIR)—an adult female horse

reining (RAYN-ing)—an event where riders guide their horses through spins, sliding stops, and other exercises

rodeo (ROH-dee-oh)—a competition in which people ride horses and bulls and rope cattle

sorrel (SOR-uhl)—a red-brown color

steer (STEER)—a young male bull

Thoroughbred (THUHR-oh-bred)—a breed of horse raised for racing

withers (WITH-urs)—the top of a horse's shoulders; a horse's height is measured from the ground to the withers.

Read More

Presnall, Judith Janda. *Rodeo Animals.* Animals with Jobs. San Diego: Kidhaven Press, 2003.

Price, Steven D. *The Kids' Book of the American Quarter Horse.* New York: Lyons Press, 1999.

Sherman, Josepha. *Barrel Racing.* Rodeo. Chicago: Heinemann, 2000.

Internet Sites

FactHound offers a safe, fun way to find Internet sites related to this book. All of the sites on FactHound have been researched by our staff.

Here's how:

1. Visit *www.facthound.com*
2. Type in this special code **0736837647** for age-appropriate sites. Or enter a search word related to this book for a more general search.
3. Click on the **Fetch It** button.

FactHound will fetch the best sites for you!

Index